Play Better GOLF

RENTON LAIDLAW

Series editor: Paul Wade

PELHAM BOOKS
LONDON

Produced by
Breslich & Foss
Golden House
28-31 Great Pulteney Street
London W1R 3DD

Concept: Team Wade
Fitness Consultant: Gordon Richards MBE
Design: Roger Daniels
Photographs: Phil Sheldon
Cover Photograph: Tommy Hindley
Editor: Judy Martin

First published in Great Britain by
Pelham Books Ltd
44 Bedford Square
London WC1B 3DP
1986

British Library Cataloguing in Publication Data

Laidlaw, Renton
    Play better golf : 50 star tips.
    1. Golf
    I. Title   II. Richards, Gordon
    796.352'3   GV965

    ISBN 0-7207-1684-5

Typeset by Lineage Ltd, Watford
Originated and printed by
Toppan Printing Co. (S) Pte. Ltd., Singapore

Contents

Introduction

The beauty of golf is its variety. Unlike tennis or swimming, soccer or squash, there is no uniformity in the surroundings of the game – no one golf course is like any other. Almost every country boasts at least eighteen holes for the benefit of residents and visitors alike. If you play golf, you can find a game and make new acquaintances everywhere you go.

Golf really does transcend frontiers. In the past 20 years, this British sport, widely popularized by American players, has produced stars from such varied cultures as Spain (Seve Ballesteros), Japan (Isao Aoki) and Australia (Greg Norman). Every year new names from newer golfing nations present their challenge. Television transmission of the great golf tournaments strengthens this common interest all around the world. I myself have written for *The London Standard* and broadcast from all five continents, cataloguing the achievements of the international players

Golf is my business and my pleasure. As an avid amateur player and one occasionally invited to play alongside the greats in pro-am tournaments, I can still appreciate the expertise of the stars and identify the common faults which less practised players often make. With the aid of 50 excellent photographs by Phil Sheldon, one of Britain's leading specialists, I have explained how the stars play both the classic and the unorthodox shots that represent the versatility of the international game today.

Fitness consultant Gordon Richards has trained athletes in a wide range of sports, taking them to Olympic and World Championship gold medals. For this book he has created a challenging but not time-consuming exercise plan designed not only to keep you in peak condition, but also to help you improve your game and avoid common sporting injuries.

My thanks go to Paul Wade, Series Editor, for practical assistance and encouragement in preparing this handbook, and to my respected colleague Peter Dobereiner, for invaluable advice. All in all, I hope the book really will enable you to 'Play Better Golf' and increase your enjoyment of this fascinating game.

Severiano Ballesteros
Address position

Golf fans around the world thrill to the power
through the green and silky touch on the
putting surface of Severiano Ballesteros, the
world's Number One golfer. Seve's colleagues
admire him, too, not only for his determination,
his courage and undoubted talent, but also for
his attention to basics – his set-up prior to
playing any shot is superb.

His address for this drive is as near to
perfection as it could be. Notice the lack of
tension, the relaxed state he is in before
beginning his backswing. Everything looks
comfortable and natural – as well it might be for
someone who has been playing most of his life.
The ex-caddy from Pedrena in northern Spain
was once so poor he had only one secondhand
club – now he is a golfing millionaire, winning
around the world with ease. His technique –
solid and reliable – is worth its weight in gold.

COMMON FAULTS

● Creating
unnecessary tension
by gripping the club
too tightly.

● Not taking enough
care in lining up the
shot, resulting in a
ball driven wide of the
fairway.

ACTION ANALYSIS

● When taking up your stance or
address, it is best to use a regular
routine. Most professionals, having
teed up the ball on a reasonably high
tee, set the driver behind the ball
holding the club only in the left hand.
The right hand is then folded onto the
grip.

● Check you are not standing too far
from the ball. If you feel you are over-
stretching, move slightly nearer. The
ball is normally positioned at a point
opposite the left heel and the feet are
spread about shoulder width apart,
although this is a matter for personal
preference.

● In this case, Ballesteros's feet are
lined up in a natural position. The
lines through toes, hips and
shoulders all point towards his target.
If his left foot were a little further
back the stance would be open; if it
were slightly forward the stance
would be closed.

● The club should be an extension of
the straight left arm – as is clearly
seen in Seve's address. His head is
behind the ball and because his right
hand is below the left on the shaft of
the club, his right shoulder is lower
than his left. From this position he
can complete a full shoulder turn and
has the basis of a sound drive over
260 yards (240 metres) – or more

Nick Faldo

Vardon grip

Nick Faldo has reshaped his swing over a 12-month period – an operation designed to give him more consistency in his long game. It has meant an anxious readjustment period for this British golfer, who first took up the game because he so enjoyed watching the top players on television. This shot from behind shows his Vardon grip perfectly and is a good indication of why he is among the world's top players.

Most golfers today use what is commonly known as the Vardon grip – named for Harry Vardon, six-times winner of the British Open, who perfected it. Vardon held the club with the little finger of his right hand overlapping the first finger of the left hand. For most golfers it is very comfortable, but if your hands are small, you might find the interlocking grip more suitable. In this the first finger of the left hand and little finger of the right interlock to provide more control.

In this excellent action shot of the talented Faldo, his hips have turned out of the way to make room for his arms to swing the club through to a perfect high finish.

ACTION ANALYSIS

● Faldo's example shows a sensible technique for gaining extra control. The club is held a little below the end of the shaft rather than at the top of the leather or rubber grip.

● The correct placing of the left hand on the shaft should have the club resting across the base of the fingers with two knuckles showing and the 'V' formed by the thumb and pad of the forefinger pointing over the right shoulder.

● The right hand is cupped over the left thumb with the little finger resting lightly between the first two fingers of the left hand – Vardon style! A grip in which the right hand is too strong, that is, rotated too far under the shaft, will cause you to hook. If it is too weak you will slice.

● It will pay you to make sure your grip is correct every time. Always hold the club lightly to avoid causing unnecessary tension.

Jack Nicklaus
Reverse overlap grip

Jack Nicklaus, winner of 17 major professional titles on the world circuit since 1961, is seen here on the green putting with a reverse overlap grip. In this the left forefinger rests on top of the right-hand fingers, the reason being to get all the fingers of the dominant right hand onto the grip and to reduce any tendency to a breaking of the wrists in the putting stroke. Elsewhere on the course Nicklaus uses the interlocking grip (see previous page) which has proved highly successful for him.

Some golfers prefer an even two-handed grip, also known as the baseball grip, in which all the fingers of both hands are on the shaft of the club. This provides firmer contact for long shots, but this grip makes integrated use of the hands more difficult. The object is to get both hands operating as one, and anything that makes this a more effortful task can hardly be recommended. At the end of the day, as with so much in golf, it all comes down to personal preference, but just remember that your hands and grip are your only contact with the club. Get this wrong and your swing will be wrong, and your score will suffer. Too many people do not get maximum enjoyment from the game because they do not take care about the grip.

Note how many golfers wear a glove on the left hand to ensure good contact with the club grip. This is particularly useful for full shots, though not always necessary in putting.

Not everyone agrees, but it is generally considered that the left-hand guides the club during the swing and the right provides the power at impact. Since the whole action should be thought of as one flowing movement, do not be too conscious of these individual functions. Keep everything as simple as you can.

COMMON FAULTS

● A weak grip which leaves the left wrist less firm than it should be.

● An excessively tight grip which restricts the free swinging of the club. Think of the club as an extension of your arm.

Hale Irwin

The swing

Hale Irwin is a classic swinger of the golf club. Twice winner of the US Open, over tough Winged Foot in 1974 and at Inverness, Toledo in 1979, Irwin has a faultless technique.

His take-away is smooth and initially in one piece. In this picture he has reached the precise moment to cock his wrists. Having achieved this important initial movement, he is set to rotate his upper body.

COMMON FAULTS

● Cocking the wrists too quickly at take-away.

● Failure to take the club-head back on the inside.

Could you ask for a better top-of-the-backswing position? Irwin has made a full shoulder turn, the source of much power in the swing, and is looking at the ball over his left shoulder. His weight at this point is on the inside of his right foot as he prepares to change swing direction and pull down into the ball. Note how precisely the club points towards the intended target.

COMMON FAULTS

● Inadequate shoulder turn and failure to complete the backswing.

● Failure to initiate the downswing with a transfer of weight from right foot to left.

Keeping his head perfectly steady throughout the swing sequence, Irwin has unwound smoothly to hit the ball on the downswing with his 3-wood. With a driver he would have made contact on the upswing and would consequently have played the shot with the ball further forward into the stance. There has been smooth transference of weight on to the left foot.

COMMON FAULTS

● Body swaying laterally into the ball, causing loss of power at the strike.

● A tendency to slow up at contact instead of maintaining hand speed.

With his head still well down and his eyes fixed firmly on the spot from which he hit the ball, Irwin has followed through beautifully. The power and impetus of the shot is pulling him round to face his target and he has achieved maximum power by proper rolling of the hands at impact. Many amateurs decelerate at impact, blocking the shot and sending the ball off to the right.

COMMON FAULTS

● Failure to roll wrists, causing loss of power and distance.

● Premature lifting of the head, through anxiety to see the result of the shot.

Bernhard Langer
Short iron

Bernhard Langer has a well-deserved reputation as the most precise hitter of an iron shot in golf. His long irons are particularly impressive but here this fine golfer shows how good he is with the short irons as well. The picture was taken at the US Masters in 1984 – the year before Langer conquered the course, staggered the field and surprised the CBS commentary team, who did not even know how to pronounce his name properly. They know now!

As in all his golf shots, Langer is showing maximum concentration. Indeed, he shares with Nicklaus and Ballesteros the crucial ability to shut out all distractions and regularly makes birdies with precision shots like the one he is playing here.

COMMON FAULTS
● Rushing the shot, beginning the hit from the top of the backswing.

● Initiating the backswing with a tilting of the shoulders rather than a turning motion.

ACTION ANALYSIS

● For a man of his size – 5ft 9in (1.75m) – Langer swings the club on a flatter-than-usual plane. It is normally easier for men of his build to swing on a steeper arc. Shorter players generally use the flatter swing.

● Bernhard's style is a little different from the rest, but he generates great power in the hitting area, as can be seen from the picture. His left arm is perfectly straight and the right elbow tucked into his side in copybook style. The club-head is about to reach maximum acceleration as he prepares to hit and it will be moving at extraordinary speed when it hits the ball on the downswing.

● Judging from the position of his feet, he has opened his stance a little to facilitate a cutting action through the ball – quite normal for a 'fading' shot, that is, one that moves from left to right.

● His head is just behind the ball but his body has superb control as his hips begin to rotate to make the strike. Control comes from total confidence, and confidence is helped considerably by being completely at ease with the rhythm and tempo of the swing. One of the most destructive movements in golf is the lateral movement of the head, but there is no suggestion of head movement on this shot and the ball almost certainly fell close to the stick.

David Graham
Medium iron

Not everyone swings in the same way, but all the great players have one important thing in common. They get the club-head back square to hit the ball. Australian David Graham, now permanently based in Texas, has one of top golf's more stilted or mechanical swings, but it works well for him. A US Open title at Merion in 1981 and a US PGA title three years earlier are testimony to that. In addition, he has won around the world with, at times, considerable ease. It is reward for long hours spent on the practice ground – there really is no substitute for practising sensibly.

Graham has worked out a technique which suits him – and that is the key. Backing up his technical ability is a fierce competitive spirit and a touch on the greens that has broken many an opponent's challenge.

ACTION ANALYSIS

● The medium iron shot which David Graham has just played would have satisfied anyone. Note how his head has remained at the address position even though the rest of his body has bowed through. He may not have turned his hips towards the target as much as normal, but the left leg is nicely braced to take the impact of the shot.

● It looks as if Graham is using a 6-iron and his body turn is greater with the longer power club than with those he uses for precision work. The shot also illustrates very clearly how good his hand action is. Above all, his timing has been excellent, clipping the ball first, then taking a very shallow divot.

● The great advantage the pro has over the amateur is the ability through regular practice and sound knowledge of his swing to keep repeating the same action consistently. With such a shot the Australian most probably managed to spin the ball close to the hole for another birdie chance. It is the typically aggressive action shot of a golfer who once played left-handed before switching to the more usual right-handed method. His natural left-handedness has been, in fact, an advantage because golf, although a two-handed game, is a mainly left-sided action with the left arm guiding the club.

Greg Norman
Long iron

Australian Greg Norman is a golfer who plays
and wins around the world. Although he has
never won a major his game is always
impressive not least because of his awesome
length. The blond Queenslander is arguably the
second longest driver and 1-iron player in the
world, behind only Britain's Open champion
Sandy Lyle.

As can be seen in this shot of Norman
playing the European Open at Sunningdale, he
uses his height — 6ft 1in (1.8m) — well,
standing up to the ball instead of crouching
over the shot. His superb fitness is also a key
factor to his success on the well-watered
fairways of US country-club courses. He carries
the ball a long way in the air and that, of course,
is vital in the States where the ball does not roll
on the usually softer ground.

ACTION ANALYSIS

● Like all great players, Greg
Norman makes even the longest iron
shot look easy. Few amateurs use the
1-iron with its very straight face
because they find it too difficult to
play. The straighter the face of the
club, the more precise the hit has to
be. You might prefer instead to take a
3-wood, the face of which has
enough loft to inspire confidence.

● Norman swings fully on a wide arc
to build up the power needed for a
big hit, with an upright swing typical
of a man of his size. At all times
playing with a smooth tempo and
rhythm, Norman has just made
square contact with the club-head on
the ball. The picture illustrates clearly
the fundamental theory that the
club-head, having been delivered
back to the ball, makes contact on
the final fraction of the downswing,
catching the ball before the turf. The
ball is well on its way towards the
target as Norman takes a shallow
divot.

● Remember that if you want to hit
an extra-long shot and are not as well
equipped to do so as Greg Norman,
the last thing you should be thinking
about is trying to generate more
swing speed and hit the ball even
harder. That will prove counter-
effective. To hit a really big Norman-
like iron, swing even more slowly and
easily than usual and concentrate on
making precise contact with the
sweet spot on the club-head.

Nancy Lopez
Fairway wood

This excellent action picture of top woman golf professional Nancy Lopez shows her hitting a wood from the fairway – and there is no doubting her superb technique. One of the most endearing personalities on tour, with a ready wit and regular smile, Nancy proves that to hit the ball a long way it is not necessary to be a tall, heavy muscleman. She achieves her length as much by skilful timing as by the power of the hit.

The style of this superstar golfer from New Mexico differs in one important respect from that of most other players, including Jack Nicklaus (see following page). She cocks her wrists on the backswing far more quickly than most. Her wrists are broken just after take-away, whereas Nicklaus, for example, keeps the take-away in one piece almost to waist height. Nancy's method works well for her, but it is not one to be deliberately copied. She is not, of course, the only golfer with an idiosyncratic swing – think of US golfers Gay Brewer with his flying right elbow (the result of an accident) and Doug Sanders, with a swing so short, it's said that he could practise in a telephone booth. The acid test is not 'Does it look good?', but rather 'Does it work?'

COMMON FAULTS

● Quitting at the point of contact instead of completing the swing.

● Dropping the left shoulder and the head, making proper contact with the ball impossible because of the ruined swing plane.

ACTION ANALYSIS

● Nancy's hips are turning well, she has transferred her weight to her left side, but her head is still behind the ball. She focuses on the ball with both eyes. Her hands are rolling well at impact, her left arm is straight and her right elbow tucked tightly into her body.

● From this position Nancy would have hit her fairway wood about 200 yards (184 metres). Note that she is using the Vardon overlapping grip with a slightly weaker than normal left hand, placed on top of the shaft rather than alongside.

Jack Nicklaus
The drive

Jack Nicklaus has rewritten the record books since turning professional in 1961. Since then he has won 70 times on the US tour alone, five times been Player of the Year and, even if he is now reducing his schedule, his record will be tough to beat.

Nicklaus's career as a player has been one of high consistency maintained by an enthusiastic desire not only to be Number One but to remain at the top. Behind his success story are long, punishing hours spent on the practice ground. Nicklaus has worked hard for what he has achieved, helped by a tremendously competitive nature. Arguably the greatest golfer ever, Nicklaus really is in a class by himself.

Now Nicklaus is far more busy designing golf courses – many of which are being used to stage the great golf tournaments in the United States. This picture was taken at Shoal Creek, designed by Nicklaus and venue of the US PGA championship in 1984. It shows clearly the inside-to-out swing pattern of the drive.

COMMON FAULTS

● Sliding instead of turning into the shot.

● Keeping the arms, legs and body muscles far too tense throughout the swing.

ACTION ANALYSIS

● Some people might argue that Jack Nicklaus has a flying right elbow – but not in this shot. If it was flying on the backswing it is most certainly tucked into the body as he comes into the hitting area. You could not get a postcard between his right elbow and chest.

● There is no question of Nicklaus beginning the hit at the top of the downswing. He waits the perfect moment to whip the club-head round and into the back of the ball – which is teed up an inch-and-a-half (4cm) off the ground every time. His lower body, with the knees nicely flexed and the hips ready to turn through the shot, is relaxed but steady enough to eliminate the common amateur fault of swaying into the shot and losing power.

● The noticeable turning of Nicklaus's head at address is deliberate on his part. While others might focus on the ball with the right eye (or, like Nancy Lopez, with both eyes), Nicklaus uses his dominant left eye for focusing. Whichever you use, just make sure you keep it on the ball long enough to see the hit.

Lee Trevino
Open stance

Supermax Lee Trevino has a method very different from everyone else on the US circuit. Indeed, he himself has suggested his style of play with an open stance differs from that of 99.9 per cent of all other players. When he addresses the ball, he is positioned well ahead of the conventional spot and the imaginary lines through his shoulders, hips and feet form a relatively wide angle to the target.

This unconventional method has not stopped Trevino winning two Open championships in Britain, two US Opens and two US PGA titles – the last in 1984. He may have lost two fortunes in unlucky business ventures, but has always bounced back. Now the breezy Trevino is playing and commentating on the US tour, more than ever involved in the golf scene.

ACTION ANALYSIS

● In the conventional open stance, the left foot is positioned a little further back from the right, giving freedom but also control in the swing. In Trevino's unique open stance, he is standing aligned at 30 degrees or more left of the target, but with his club lined up towards the target.

● Trevino does this in order to more easily take the club-head back outside the flight path. Most other golfers move inside the flight path on the backswing, but Trevino only moves inside after extending his take-away outside the swing path. This allows room for the club to loop inside where he wants it as he begins the downswing. His method only works because of this loop. If he brought the club-head back to the ball on the same outside trajectory as the take-away, he would cut every shot because he would clip the ball with the club-head moving right to left instead of squarely behind the ball.

● In order to get a good lateral (sideways) movement of the hips, Trevino makes a very full shoulder turn. Take care if you want to try the Trevino method. If you do not loop back inside and make a smooth lateral slide of the hips, you are in real trouble.

● One final point to note: Trevino has kept the club-head moving towards the target longer than usual before turning inside, round and up, extending his left arm and dropping his right shoulder under his chin.

Neil Coles
Closed stance

Neil Coles, now in his 50s, has been one of Britain's most consistent performers for 25 years, helped by a smooth swing and a normally even temperament. In addition to playing, Coles has spent much time in recent years helping to set up the European golf circuit.

Many younger players would love to have a swing like that of 'Old King Coles', who is a wizard with a wedge. In this shot he appears to be playing off a slightly closed stance in order to draw the ball – move it right to left. He is a golfer whose lazy action is glorious to watch and superbly effective, a classic swinger of the club. He is at all times swinging within himself, that is, with a controlled and comfortable action. This gives him a margin on occasion to overstretch a shot in order to gain an extra 10 to 15 yards (9 to 14 metres).

COMMON FAULTS
● Letting go of the club at the top of the swing – hold on!
● Dipping the left shoulder instead of rotating it.

ACTION ANALYSIS

● In the closed stance, used to draw the ball, the left foot is positioned slightly ahead of the right. Neil Coles has here made a beautiful swing and at this point his weight is on the right leg. The transference of weight to his left leg will begin when he is ready to bring the club down from that excellent top-of-the-swing position.

● The club is pointing directly at the target and Coles's shoulders have turned so well that his back is also towards the intended target. His stance is comfortably shoulder-width.

● Note how well he is concentrating on keeping his head still and his eye on the ball. Anxiety is the enemy of many an amateur golfer, causing a tendency to rush or snatch a shot and jerk the head up before hitting the ball in an effort to see where it will go. A smooth swing and total concentration on the ball, as demonstrated by Neil Coles, are the elements which allow you to make a clean, solid hit.

● Coles has one idiosyncracy which is that after impact the club twists through 90° in his hands, showing how lightly he has gripped despite the power and control of the shot.

Sandy Lyle
Iron off tee

Sandy Lyle, British Open champion of 1985, is acknowledged as one of the world's longest hitters of the golf ball. He regularly hits 280-yard (258-metre) drives and is almost as long with the 1-iron that amateurs find so difficult to use because of its straight face. In fact, Lyle often plays off the tee with his 1-iron instead of a driver or 3-wood, even on holes which are not tight drives. It does give him greater accuracy, of course, because he can control the ball so much better firing it off on a lower trajectory than is usual.

The big Scotsman, who has been playing since he was 3 years old, has a long back and broad shoulders, with powerful legs and hands to generate tremendous strength at the hitting position.

COMMON FAULTS

● Bad timing – the 1-iron must be used accurately, so swing slowly and wait for the moment to release the power.

● Teeing the ball up too high when the aim is to hit a low shot.

ACTION ANALYSIS

● Sandy Lyle's waterproof clothing shows how bad the conditions were when he played Severiano Ballesteros in the 1983 World Match-Play final at Wentworth. A full shoulder turn on the backswing and a smooth, full follow-through cannot be more restricted than when the golfer is cocooned in waterproofs, even the lightweight type Sandy is wearing here. Despite everything, he has made good contact, concentrating even harder than usual because of the unpleasant conditions. He will have made sure that the grip of his club was quite dry, to avoid letting it slip in his hands.

● Lyle's head is rock-steady. He has transferred his weight onto the left leg and as his hips turn he has plenty of room to extend through the ball and round to a high finish. The left hand, having led the club into the hitting position, has been overtaken by the right as it rolls through the shot.

● Sandy has such a natural talent that very little ever goes wrong. He is lucky that when it does, he can just head home to Hawkstone Park in the English Midlands for a lesson from the local golf professional – his father, Alex. If he is too far away he can easily talk the problem through on the telephone. It could help you to have regular check-ups from your local pro, just to make sure no recurring faults are creeping into your swing. Even the top players benefit from a regular tune-up and some sound professional advice.

Ian Woosnam
Playing to advantage

Welshman Ian Woosnam may be small in build
– he is just 5ft 4in (1.6m) tall – but he packs
quite a punch when driving the golf ball. He
can outdrive far bigger men, using his muscular
arms to good effect, as can be seen in this
picture of Woosnam in action in the 1985 PGA
Championship at the famous Wentworth West
Course.

As a rule the momentum of the swing itself
contributes to the speed and power of the shot,
but the smaller the player, the smaller the arc of
the swing. Ian's great strength is in his superb
rhythm, which is serving him well in this shot.
Strong arms and excellent timing can be used
to match the natural advantage bestowed by
height. Woosnam comes from a long line of
determined Welshmen who have not been
giants as regards physique, but have certainly
made a major impact on the European golfing
scene. Severiano Ballesteros regards Woosnam
as a golfer with a particularly effective, almost
faultless swing. There can be no greater tribute!

COMMON FAULTS

● Hitting heavy,
catching the ground
before the ball.

● Attempting a shot
unsuited to actual
physical range –
gauge distance
carefully and make a
careful choice of the
appropriate club.

ACTION ANALYSIS

● From a slightly uphill lie, Woosnam
has hit a superb shot here.
Photographer Phil Sheldon's specially
designed no-noise camera catches it
just before the club hits the ball. It is
clear that contact will be made on
the downswing.

● How well Woosnam has kept his
head firm and how expertly he is
turning his hips out of the way to help
him complete the shot. The left leg is
firm. He is clearly hitting down,
under and through with the right
shoulder set to finish underneath his
chin.

● Most smaller men swing on a flat
plane, most taller players on a steeper
trajectory, but in both cases they
would benefit from making an effort
to swing slightly more steeply if
small, and with slightly more flatness
if tall. The curve of the iron club as
Woosnam generates maximum
power gives ample evidence of the
Welshman's ability to hit on average
250 yards (230 metres) and note, too,
how he is smoothly transferring his
weight from the right to the left leg.

Ted Dexter
Feet above ball

Former Test cricketer and England captain Ted Dexter won the President's Putter, the annual New Year's Day competition held in England between members of the Oxford and Cambridge Golfing Society, in 1983 after years of trying. His victory did not come without a few moments of anxiety, including this incident when Dexter found himself halfway up a grassy bank with the ball partly buried in a tuft.

The competition has often been affected by bad weather – in the past it has been snowed off – and in 1983 there was a cruelly cold wind whipping over the links, making victory a matter not only of top quality play but of stamina as well. Dexter lacks nothing as far as fighting qualities go, but the shot he had to manufacture here was one he never needs to play at his home course of Sunningdale.

COMMON FAULTS

● Attempting a far too ambitious shot from this kind of lie.

● Shanking (hitting off the heel of the club) from the above-the-ball position.

ACTION ANALYSIS

● Some of us make golf a difficult enough game even if we are hitting every shot through the green off a level lie on a perfect surface – but it can be so much more exasperating when the ball strays off line. In a howling gale at the seaside in mid-winter, it is easy to land in the kind of trouble Ted Dexter has here, with this awkward stance above the ball. As you can see, his left foot is appreciably higher than his right, and he has had to stretch forward and down to make contact with the half-buried ball.

● Dexter has succeeded and the ball is on its way back to the comparative safety of the fairway, or even onto the green. In general, you hold the club for this kind of shot right up at the end of the grip, thus adding length, and you keep the knees well-flexed through the shot while trying to maintain balance. Dexter, however, not only had to cope with the stance but also make sure of popping the ball out of trouble. He chose instead to go down the shaft and explode the ball out with a short but effective backswing and hardly any follow-through.

● Note that the important point here was to get the ball back in play, and not to try for distance. Over-ambition on Dexter's part could have cost him victory – but he was far too shrewd to be caught out and contrived to hit the whole ball, not just the visible top half.

Stuart Reese
Uphill lie

Stuart Reese of New Zealand, who regularly plays on the European circuit, found himself in an awkward spot during the Dunhill Cup at St Andrews, Scotland, in October 1985. In the undulating ground of a seaside course, a golfer can expect to play shots up or down, whether on the fairway or in the rough. For Reese this was unusual terrain, but he showed himself equal to it.

Reese came to the one-million-dollar event at St Andrews via a most unusual putt holed for his team in the Pacific Qualifying at Hong Kong. The result of New Zealand's match with the Philippines depended on whether Reese won his game, and he did, helped by the 40-yard (37-metre) putt on the seventeenth which took 10 seconds to drop! Reese almost despaired as the ball teetered on the edge but remained above the hole. Then, as he walked towards it, the ball dropped in. He showed great fighting qualities in the pressure-packed last moments of that tie, proving again that nerve and control are of primary importance in golf. Technical skill is not always enough.

COMMON FAULTS

● Trying to scoop the ball clear of trouble – not letting the loft of the club do the work.

● From this position, hooking badly. Alter your stance to reduce the danger.

ACTION ANALYSIS

● The great danger when playing a shot in which your left foot is above the right, like Stuart Reese's here, is that you may pull the ball left of target. It is easy to do this because typically, with the bulk of the weight on the right foot, a golfer will swing rather flat around the body rather than up and round as normal. You can see how Stuart's weight is all on the right side even after he has hit the shot. He has not been able to transfer it in the usual way.

● Reese has tried to counteract this tendency to pull the ball by adopting an open stance – that is, with his left foot further back than his right – in the hope that he might be able to cut the ball clear or at least attack it from a steeper angle. We do not know where the target is in relation to the shot being played, but it is possible the toes of his feet are parallel to the line of his intended shot, which in this case would be right of the target point.

Hubert Green
Pitch to elevated green

Regular competitors in the USA have a special need to master this shot, because so many greens there are plateau-style in design. Most putting surfaces in American courses of this type are 'holding', meaning the ball does not run on, so Hubert Green could afford to go for the pin and expect the ball to check on landing. Judging from his slightly open stance, it is likely that he cut the ball up, although he does appear to have made a somewhat flatter swing than he normally uses.

Another useful approach shot is the chip and run, chased up and onto a non-plateau green that is too hard in texture to hold a high 'floater' of the kind Green played here. As always on these shots, remember to follow through and complete the shot. If you stab at it or do not complete the follow-through, you are liable to be hitting your next ball from the sand. Swing too fast at the ball and you might 'thin' it – that is, catch only the top half of the ball with the sole of the club, sending it flying over the green! Then you will be faced with playing a similar shot back.

The various approach shots are always worth practising regularly because played properly they can save you one, two or even more shots a round and, at the end of the day, it all adds up to a lower handicap.

Gillian Stewart
Chip over hazard

Few golfers have the ability to hit this attractive tenth green off the tee at the Belfry. It is a carry of over 200 yards (184 metres) to a green not only set at an angle to the tee, but also guarded by water and huge overhanging trees. It has proved possible for Greg Norman, Seve Ballesteros, Sam Torrance and Sandy Lyle to fade their tee shots through the gap, but most golfers prefer to hit an iron down to the edge of the lake and use a wedge for an approach shot intended to land close to the pin.

This is what professional woman golfer Gillian Stewart has done in the European Open, which she won as an amateur in 1984. She has placed her tee shot perfectly, leaving an easy 80-yard (73-metre) lob onto the green. Gillian would not scoop at the ball and try to help it on its way in the manner that many handicap amateurs would. This could result in a watery grave and more tension for a similar fourth shot.

Gillian has hit a full shot, allowing the loft on the club-head to do the job for which it was designed. Look how well she has come through as she turns towards the target.

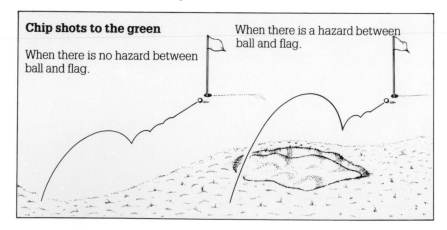

Chip shots to the green

When there is no hazard between ball and flag.

When there is a hazard between ball and flag.

Neil Coles
Fairway chip

The ability to hit good wedge shots and save strokes around the green is, in some respects, an in-born talent. The shot is all about confidence and feel, and top British golfer Neil Coles has always been a tremendous exponent of it. His ability with his wedge, and sometimes sand wedge, around the greens is equal to that of Seve Ballesteros in today's game. Coles's action has the virtue of always being executed at a leisurely pace. Nothing has been rushed in this shot.

COMMON FAULTS
● Jabbing at the shot with a restricted backswing.

● Scooping the ball, not letting the club-head do the job for which it was designed.

ACTION ANALYSIS

● The wedge shot, whether a pitch or, as shown here, a chip, is a real stroke-saver. Getting the ball close enough to the pin to hole a par putt is the object of the exercise, and Coles is a past master at it. Note how his feet are together for this shot because he will require very little body movement. His head was over the ball at address and is still over that same spot after the ball has left the club face.

● He has punched this shot, not needing to follow through, and letting the loft of the club – almost horizontal to the ground – do the work it was designed for. It lifts the ball sharply and produces backspin on landing. The club-head will continue through the shot low to the ground and you can determine just how well he has clipped the ball off the turf. There is no divot!

● His hands have been well in front of the ball throughout, characteristic of a punch shot. In the punch you have a reasonable, if shorter than usual, backwards movement, but still let the club-head swing through the shot. Although the swing is shorter the tempo remains the same as for a full swing.

● Keeping reasonably loose on this shot is vital but getting the balance of a relaxed yet firm execution is difficult and requires considerable practice. Coles often plays this shot as he strolls around his garden. He seldom, if ever, gets it wrong.

Hubert Green

Chipping from the fringe

Hubert Green from Alabama survived a death-threat when he won the US Open in 1976, which indicates how cool he can be in a crisis. In 1985, when his top-line competitive career seemed almost over, he came back brilliantly to win the US PGA at Cherry Hills in Denver, showing all his old skill at manufacturing shots through and around the greens. Here, in the 1980 US Open at Baltusrol, he produces a shot to meet the occasion to salvage his par with a chip and putt.

Green's whole technique is most unusual and distinctive – his style is such a personal one that he can easily be spotted on the course. He tends to crouch on most shots and can be bent almost double as he putts. He is proof, if it were needed, that it is not necessary to have a classic swing as long as you have a good rhythm and an action that can be repeated.

COMMON FAULTS

● Trying to putt the ball out of grass this thick. It is impossible to judge accurately how hard you should hit the ball.

● Not having the confidence to use a lofted club and hit the ball a firm blow.

ACTION ANALYSIS

● Hubert Green has opted to go right down the shaft of his wedge for more control of this shot. His hands are so far down the shaft that they are actually below the level of his knees and this helps him virtually to eliminate body movement. His aim is to drop the ball near the edge of the slick green and let it roll up to the hole, because he will get little or no backspin.

● This is one instance when it is not possible to pitch up to the flag. He has guaranteed that he will hit down and through the ball by standing in such a way that he is playing the shot not with the ball equidistant between the feet, but level with his right toe.

● The tendency of most amateurs would be to slow up in the hitting area or to 'baby' the shot, the result of inbuilt anxiety. Green has none of that! He has made firm, crisp contact, maintaining maximum concentration throughout.

● This shot is very useful for dealing with a thick collar of rough just beyond the apron of the green, a regular feature of US championship courses. But the technique Green uses here is one well worth knowing and adapting to longer shots from similar lies.

Bernhard Langer
Unusual difficulty

West Germany's Bernhard Langer was far from happy when his second shot crashed into the trees surrounding the seventeenth green at Fulford in the 1981 Benson and Hedges tournament. It is always a tight approach, but what worried Langer was that he had not seen the ball bounce clear and onto the green. He expected it to be in the long grass behind the tree, but he was wrong. The ball had stayed *up* the tree, nestling neatly in a fork in the branches.

Langer produced an unusual solution. Instead of declaring the ball unplayable he climbed the tree (with the help of spectators) and proceeded to play the ball onto the green, avoiding a penalty. It was a shot that required a short, sharp jab and a modicum of luck. It would have been easy to miss the ball altogether but Langer was equal to the task, despite the awkwardness of his stance and the extraordinary golfing hazard of trying not to fall to the ground!

Situations of this kind do arise in golf and Langer proves that nothing is impossible – but it takes a player of his calibre to produce a shot as skilful as this. For an amateur, it would be better to declare the ball unplayable, cut the loss and go for a drop (see page 72), which at least puts the ball back into play, although incurring a penalty.

Make sure you don't invite such a problem by trying to play the ball through trees. Use a lofted club to lift it high in the air and over the top of the obstacle. By the way, when you see the ball heading for the trees, keep watching to see where it lands, so you can find it again even if it is unplayable. If no-one sees it and you cannot track its position, it is necessary to drop from the point where the shot was played, thus incurring both stroke and distance penalties.

COMMON FAULTS

● Attempting an over-ambitious recovery shot which gets you into further trouble.

● Allowing irritation to get the better of you in a difficult situation and rushing into the next shot unprepared.

Andy North
Bunker play – buried ball

This brilliant shot helped Andy North to a second US Open triumph at Oakland Hills in 1985. He was hanging on to the lead coming to the end of the final round, but hit into sand at the short seventeenth. The ball was lying badly but North played the shot perfectly, made his par and went on to take the title.

The ball was well-buried in what is known as a 'poached egg' lie. The whole ball was not sitting on top of the sand – half its depth was below the surface. North's confidence and expertise under pressure saved the day.

The fear amateurs experience is the result of not having practised this shot very often. How regularly do you use the practice bunker at your club? Does the club even have a practice bunker, and if so, is it well looked after? There is nothing difficult about bunker play if you know what you are doing.

COMMON FAULTS
● Setting up wrongly, reducing your chance of a good recovery.

● Lack of regular practice, making the shot a hit-or-miss affair in play.

ACTION ANALYSIS

● In normal circumstances a golfer splashes his ball out of a sand-trap by sending the blade of the sand-wedge cutting underneath the ball. In a 'poached egg' situation, however, the ball is so badly buried that it would be impractical to dig the blade deep enough to get under the ball and through the sand, so a different technique is employed.

● Instead of opening the stance as for a normal sand shot recovery, you stand square to the ball with the club-head slightly hooded, or closed. The idea is to hit down powerfully and sharply on the sand just behind the ball, so that the steep angle of attack will make it possible for you to propel a cushion of sand and the ball on to the green. It works if you have the courage to play it.

● You will not be able to put any backspin on the ball and there is no short-cut to success with this shot. Only by experience can you learn how far behind the ball to hit, how much sand to take to get the ball on to the green. That sand, by the way, comes in different consistencies – fluffy, heavy or wet – so get to know how to play out of every sandy lie. The texture of the sand determines how far you hit behind the ball, the wetter and heavier the sand is, the closer you will hit.

Keith Fergus
Bunker shot

This excellent shot of the American golfer Keith Fergus splashing out of a sand trap is proof that the recovery is in itself not a difficult one. The professionals will sometimes hit deliberately into greenside traps because it affords them a better chance of making a birdie or par when for some reason they cannot go for the green. Yet the trap shot is one which causes particular anxiety in many an amateur's mind.

When Fergus blasted this ball out, note how perfectly balanced he was and how steeply that ball is coming out of trouble. This is the one occasion when it is essential to hit behind the ball for maximum effect – it is only on longer shots out of fairway traps (see following page) that you will want to clip the ball cleanly. Failure to follow through on a normal bunker shot could mean leaving the ball in the trap!

COMMON FAULTS
● Failure to make a full and leisurely backswing.

● Failure to follow through properly as with normal shots.

ACTION ANALYSIS

● It is clear from this picture that Keith Fergus has taken up the ideal address position with an open stance. His left foot is drawn back from the intended line of the shot and his weight has remained on his right side. When he addressed the ball (remembering that in a hazard it is not allowed to ground the club before hitting the ball) he would have had the club-head wide open with the face of the sand-iron virtually horizontal, to make it easier to cut through the sand beneath the ball.

● When playing this shot you pick the club up more sharply with a pronounced breaking of the wrists – in contrast to the normal one-piece take-away. What is vital is to take the club away slowly and deliberately and to follow through with equal conviction. Swing along the line of your toes, that is, well to the left of the target.

● The club-head enters the sand about 2 inches (5cm) behind the ball with the intention of sending it through and under the ball without touching it. The thick flange on the sand-iron will ensure the club reappears out of the sand, while the ball is thrown up onto the green on a cushion of sand.

● Instead of swinging round the body, this is one shot which demands a more upright swing and steeper angle of attack.

Sam Torrance
Length from bunker

Sometimes you can end up in a shallow trap in the fairway, as Sam Torrance has here in the 1983 Benson and Hedges tournament at Fulford in York. While some traps through the green at seaside links can be as deep as those around the putting surface, most fairway bunkers permit the luxury of a full recovery.

Torrance clearly felt he could do more than just splash out because he is using a longer iron. This takes the ball on a lower trajectory and allows distance on the shot. Sometimes the professionals even chance a wood, but this demands considerable nerve and control because of the necessity to keep the club-head from touching the sand before the hit! There is a penalty if you do.

In most instances amateurs should concentrate on getting out of the trouble rather than attempting to play a shot that any professional would find difficult. Over-ambition in golf is severely penalized and it is always wise to play the percentages.

COMMON FAULTS

● Touching the sand in the hazard on the backswing and incurring a penalty.

● Using a club with insufficient loft to clear the lip; that is, expecting too much from the shot.

ACTION ANALYSIS

● If the main aim in most bunker shots is to hit behind the ball and explode it out, this shot Sam Torrance is playing is a perfect example of the exception to that premise. Here Torrance wanted – and managed – to pick the ball cleanly out of the trap, making almost as much ground as if he had been hitting from the fairway. He could go for length because his ball was sitting up on the well-raked sand.

● The sand disturbed on this shot occurred after the strike and the ball position indicates how expertly he played it. The shot needed nerve and talent – two ingredients not lacking in Torrance's make-up. He has used a slightly open blade, playing with a resonably straight-faced club, to help cut the ball up and out of trouble. Once again he is clearly holding the club down the shaft a bit more than normal to help with his control. It is not the shot he could have attempted had his ball been half-buried or if the bunker had had a steeper lip – but he made good use of the opportunity afforded him. Note the firmness of his head through the shot.

Sam Torrance
Bunker play – wet sand

Sam Torrance hit into this waterlogged bunker and was unable to play out because there was no spot in it dry enough on which to drop the ball. This could have been done under the casual water rule, which covers a temporary water hazard caused by flooding. In the circumstances, Torrance has employed the unplayable rule and has dropped behind the trap on the line along which the ball entered the bunker. Had he been able to drop inside the bunker he would not have been penalized but getting total relief from the hazard does, unhappily for Torrance, mean he incurs a penalty shot. He counted himself unlucky on this occasion.

He has had to play a rather awkward shot with a downhill lie and has used a lofted club, taken back on a steeper than usual trajectory because of the slope of the land. The weight is all on the left foot, the stance is open to curb the tendency to overswing and make it easier to hit through on line to the target. Sam has cut the ball up over the trouble and onto the green.

COMMON FAULTS

● Trying to scoop up the ball by flicking the wrists, instead of letting the club face do the work.

● Snatching the shot and losing length, so the ball falls back into the water.

Tom Kite
Uphill bunker

Tom Kite is known with justification as 'Mr Consistency' on the US tour, but it is an unhappy reflection on his successful career and impeccable sportsmanship that he has been unable to win a major title. He has had his chances, of course, but perhaps he has tried too hard at the crucial moments and landed, as he

ACTION ANALYSIS

● When Tom Kite landed in this Winged Foot bunker he knew he had little chance of going directly for the flag, so he quickly decided his only option was to get the ball on the green and hope to hole a long putt for par. To try for the pin could have resulted in his burying the ball in an even more difficult spot under the lip from where it might well have been unplayable. What the professionals are so good at is not throwing away shots and Kite certainly took no chances here.

● The object of his explosion shot was to pop the ball up in the air almost vertically and let it drop onto the green firmly enough to hold its position. Golf, it has been said by many, was never meant to be a fair game. It tests the patience of a player and, not least, his control when things are going wrong. Kite could justifiably feel hard done by here but he retained control of his emotions and used his brain to try to retrieve an unhappy situation. He thought the shot through.

did in the US Open at Winged Foot in 1984, not just in trouble but in serious trouble.

This time he has hit short and wide of the pin, but his bunker shot is made more difficult by the fact he is under the lip and cannot therefore go for the flag.

Howard Clark
Bunker play – downhill lie

For Yorkshireman Howard Clark, this bunker shot at the short tenth at the Belfry, headquarters of the British PGA (Professional Golfer's Association), posed no problems. Although faced with a downhill lie in the sand, the trap had little or no rim and Howard could easily splash out with a firm but nevertheless flowing shot. Many amateurs, conscious that they must dig into and through the sand to get the ball clear, play a nervous jab, dig in too deep and are unable to follow through. The result is that the ball hops forward either to the fringe of the green or just drops down ahead of them still in the sand.

Clark has played the shot perfectly, having opened his stance and angled the club face until it was almost horizontal. The club-head has skimmed through and underneath the ball, while Clark has his weight on the left foot.

Clark is at the back of the bunker and is using a sand wedge to play the shot. In a similar situation on the greenside of a bunker which has no lip, it would be possible just to putt the ball out. This is an example of the versatility of your selection of clubs – the putter is not exclusively for use on the green. Hit slightly harder than usual to allow the ball to pass over the soft sand and a short fringe before reaching the green. To gauge the stroke, visualize the pin as being about 30 per cent farther away than it actually is.

Bunker play demands a certain technique, or rather techniques, depending on the lie of the ball, the texture of the sand and the design of the bunker, so take time out to practise the varied shots that can make par saving much more possible.

Arnold Palmer
Bunker power

This dramatic shot shows the legendary Arnold Palmer in a bit of trouble at Oakmont, the renowned Championship course at Pittsburg, Pennsylvania. He is in the famous church pews – a row of parallel, grassy-banked bunkers which have ruined a good many cards. It might be surprising that a player of Palmer's class has found his way into this unusual hazard, but he has had some luck in that the ball has landed in a trough of sand rather than on one of the grassy ridges where he would have been faced with a difficult shot requiring an awkward stance and would have been unable to get any distance. But even from the sand, the shot Palmer had to play precluded his gaining much distance.

You are unlikely to come up against a hazard as daunting as the church pews, but when you are in a spot of trouble the important point is to consider very carefully all the options open to you before you commit yourself to a course of action. Palmer elected on this occasion to play on towards the green, but he might just as well have played out sideways to get back onto the fairway and clear of trouble.

Severiano Ballesteros
Putting stance

Seve Ballesteros is not only a great golfer, he is in addition a superb putter. He made an unforgettable birdie putt on the last green of the Old Course at St Andrews in 1984 to make absolutely sure of his second British Open win, his first at the home of golf. He coaxed the ball into the hole on that occasion as he has done so often in the past en route to well over 40 victories world-wide.

They still talk about his incredibly brave putting on the fiercely fast, frighteningly steep greens at Augusta, Georgia, where he has won two Green Jackets. Having the nerve to stay cool on the most difficult of putting surfaces is an important aspect of Ballesteros's mastery, but then he is something of a genius in whose hands a golf club, be it driver, wedge or putter, looks incredibly natural. His putting will hopefully help him to win in the near future the title he now most wants – the US Open.

ACTION ANALYSIS

● There are hundreds of putting techniques but Ballesteros is in the classic mould. His shoulders, hips and feet are square to the line of the putt, in just the way that he sets up for a drive. Here he is selecting the line of the putt and having aligned the blade of his putter, he will eliminate this element from his mind to concentrate entirely on the pace of the putt.

● When Jack Nicklaus putts he picks out an imaginary spot on the green in front of the ball on his chosen line to the cup, but Seve pictures the whole putt, taking the club as far forward through the shot as he took it back.

He does not jab the way Gary Player does, neither does he putt pendulum-style. Seve has remarkable touch, holding the club firmly enough not to drop it, but loosely enough to maximize the sensitivity of his fingers and eradicate any forearm tension.

● In the old days many golf stars used a type of putting action in which they broke the wrists, but now most players keep the hands and arms firm throughout the stroke. Certainly Ballesteros does, using, as we see clearly here, the reverse overlap grip with the lightest of pressure.

Graham Marsh

Putting accuracy

Graham Marsh, the far-travelled Australian, follows through quite noticeably on his putts. With the ball well on its way towards the hole on this long effort Marsh, whose head has been perfectly still through the shot, has turned only at the last second to check if he did get the line and the pace right.

He is using a centre-shafted putter here, but there are other types – blade putters, where the shaft joins the club-head at the heel and mallet-headed putters with, as the name implies, a much bulkier head.

Only you can decide which putter works best for you and having found the right club you might stick with it for years. It is the club in the bag you use most of all and can get most attached to, but it is fair to point out that becoming a good putter with good 'feel' comes only from regular practice. When you choose a putter, try out different types, not only in the professional's shop, but also outside on the practice putting green, if he will let you.

A number of golfers, including Marsh's colleague from New Zealand, Bob Charles, circle a hole on the practice green with 12 balls at different distances and do not leave until they have holed all 12 in a row! A practice green should have the same good surface as the greens on the course, and when you practise putting don't just knock the ball around casually – line up every shot as if it were the real thing and make each one count.

One hindrance to good putting is an indecision in both grip and method as you attempt to remain relaxed. Some amateurs adopt not a relaxed grip and technique, but a sloppy one. Note how Marsh's putting style is relaxed but still firm.

Bernhard Langer
Alternative grips

Not many top golfers use two putting grips but
Bernhard Langer does. He putts with a
traditional right-hand-below-left for the shorter
putts and uses a left-hand-below-right for the
longer ones. He has no fixed rule regarding the
point at which he switches grips, just doing
whatever he feels comfortable with at the time.
However, a rough guide would show he uses the
grip illustrated here for shorter putts and reverts
to a conventional grip for approach putting.

Langer hit upon this means of solving his
putting problems when his career was in
jeopardy early in 1981 after he caught a severe
bout of the putting jitters – the so-called 'yips'
normally suffered by older players. He was so
uncertain on the greens he often three-putted,
sometimes four-putted. He missed from
embarassingly short range so often that some
people anticipated he might have to quit tour
play altogether – but Langer coolly analysed the
situation, convinced himself he was not a poor
putter and beat the problem through sheer guts
and determination. Obviously it took him some
time to get used to his two putting methods,
but now he is one of the most consistent putters
whichever grip he uses!

Langer's split method was thought to be a
weakness in his game which could prevent him
from winning a major title, but he proved the
theory wrong by winning the 1985 US Masters
on the glassy greens of Augusta, the severest
test of short game nerve. On the European tour
in 1985 he averaged 29.5 putts a round,
meaning that he achieved 26 single putts in 72
holes. The fact that he was the World's Number
One player in the same year proves the
importance of accurate putting in the game as
a whole.

Gary Player
Putting with a jab

South Africa's Gary Player is often referred to as the king of bunker play. He does get down in two from sand traps more often than most, but not just because of the precision of his bunker recoveries. Having got out of the sand, he usually raps in the par-saving or sometimes birdie putts from long range.

One of the most positive men in golf, Player crouches over the ball, stands knock-kneed and uses a distinctly jabbing method. When he tried a year or two ago to switch to a more flowing action, he lost his touch and quickly reverted to his old style. He putts well on any pace of green, including the fast greens of the US Masters tournaments which are as slickly surfaced as marble and demand the firmest nerve from the players. No player concentrates harder on his shots. It almost seems at times as if Player is willing the ball in – not that he will see it drop! He will only hear it fall into the cup, because he will keep his head down throughout the putting stroke and for a few seconds afterwards.

Putting is half the game in golf. It is apparent that all the top players have different skills and methods in putting, but the important elements are to plot the right line and hit the ball at the right strength. Make sure of the line before worrying about the pace of the putt.

The speed of the green can be measured with a device known as a stimpmeter in which a ball is rolled down a shute at a given angle and onto the green. The relative speed is determined by the distance it travels on the green. For example, if the ball rolls 12 feet (3.6 metres), the rating would be 12. The normal green speed is 8 or 9.

Isao Aoki
An unusual putting style

Top Japanese golfer Isao Aoki has a most unusual putting style – one he adopted in peculiar circumstances. As you can see, Aoki holds his hands really low in at his knees and hits the ball with the heel end of the putter, holding the toe of the club off the ground.

One day early in his career, Aoki turned up to play an exhibition match without clubs and had to borrow a set. The shafts were too long for him and he had to adapt his putting style to cope. He could have chosen to lay the head of the club flat on the ground and stand more upright than he would normally do, but he preferred instead to maintain his crouched stance, even if it meant striking the ball virtually off the heel of the putter. It worked. That day he holed everything and decided to stick with a longer shafted putter and a method that has won him several millions around the world.

In this picture, Aoki has just hit the ball, but it is clear that he was putting with the ball slightly ahead of his left toe. His weight is equally distributed and he is using the traditional Vardon-style overlapping grip in preference to the reverse overlap favoured by so many golfers.

Andy Bean
Reading the green

Big Andy Bean may be a powerfully long hitter, but he has a gentle touch on the greens. Here he is studying the line of a putt on the small but undulating greens of Winged Foot near New York, assessing how much the putt will break and in what direction.

Seldom is a putt straight, but judging the borrow of it can be more difficult if the grass is grainy. In some countries the grass grows not vertically, but horizontally in one direction which affects the roll of the ball. Downgrain, the ball will travel much faster than usual; into the grain it will roll much more slowly. Across the grain a 20-foot (6-metre) putt may be deflected 12 inches (30cm), even swerving uphill at times. There is generally little or no grain on English courses, but golfers enjoying sunshine golf in Florida, Spain or South Africa must look out for this problem.

Most professional golfers will study the line of their putts from all four directions to give themselves the best chance of making birdies. Sometimes – and Bean is an example – a player will hold up his putter like a plumb line to assess the amount of slope across which the putt is to be made. No artificial aids can be used, of course, such as a spirit level. That is against the rules.

Remember, having chosen your line, putt positively along it. Lack of commitment often causes putts to be missed that ought not to have been!

Peter Jacobsen
Dropping the ball

Problems for Peter Jacobsen, the popular American Ryder Cup player, who has hit into trouble in the ferns on this British course. He has elected to 'drop out' under penalty, a method of putting the ball back into play. Supervising the procedure is John Paramor, top European tour administrator.

The player's driver, the longest shafted club in the bag, is used to measure a club length or two club lengths from the original site of the ball. If for some reason relief is given without penalty, the golfer is entitled to drop the ball within one club length, but no nearer to the hole. If incurring a one-shot penalty, two club lengths are allowed. The ball may roll a further two club lengths after hitting the ground – again, of course, no nearer to the hole.

Note the way Jacobsen is dropping the ball from almost shoulder height. This method was agreed in the last rules revision as being fairer and more precise than the previous procedure of dropping the ball back into play over the shoulder.

If after two attempts at dropping the ball you are not able to prevent it from rolling nearer to the hole, or if it runs further than the two club lengths allowed, you are permitted to place it at the appropriate spot of maximum relief.

Tom Watson

Deep rough

Professionals do sometimes hit off line and if it is in the British Open, it is a fair bet they will find themselves in deep rough. Tom Watson is the golfer in trouble here at Royal St George's: significantly, he has not won an Open on this south-east England course – although he has won the title five times.

Tom and caddy Alfie Fyles had five minutes to search for the ball, and note how gingerly they are treading. If either of them stepped on the ball there would be another penalty. Try to get an accurate mark on where the ball has gone when you see it heading for the rough, to give yourself a chance of finding it in good time. Also, you will incur a distance penalty if you fail to find it at all, being required to hit another ball from the spot where you hit and lost the first!

When Watson's ball was found there was little he could do but smash it out with a wedge back onto the fairway, as if from a bunker. There is no chance of making useful distance with a shot from deep rough, because of the grass clinging to the club-head as you play the shot.

Tom Watson
Back against the wall

This is surely one of the most famous walls in golf – behind the seventeenth green at the Old Course, St Andrews. In the 1984 Open, Tom Watson has just overshot the green and is about to drop a shot to par – a crucial shot because ahead the cheers are ringing out for a Seve Ballesteros birdie on the last green. At this point Watson realises that his chance of equalling Harry Vardon's six Open victories record has gone. His back to the wall challenge has failed!

Watson has in fact been a little unlucky. His ball has flown the plateau green, hit the tarmac road that runs behind it and bounced so close to the wall that the American from Kansas City has no backswing at all. He has no room to lob the ball back on to the narrow green. Instead, using hardly any backswing, he has punched it forward with a mid-iron, hoping the ball will hit the upslope of the plateau, pop up in the air and then drop down softly beside the pin. It is a shot that requires a fair modicum of luck – and Watson did not get in on this occasion. The ball hit the bank all right, but finally came to rest too far away from the pin to give him a realistic chance of holing the putt.

Even more unlucky than Watson are those players who land up so close to the wall that they have no room to swing at all. One alternative is to try flicking the ball clear on a line parallel with the wall, a shot which does allow you a backswing and follow-through, although away from the pin.

Another line of action would be to do what Jack Nicklaus once did – hit the ball hard against the wall and rebound it out of trouble to a spot where it is possible to play a normal shot. If you try this, watch the ball does not hit you on the rebound – you will be penalized.

Curtis Strange
Playing out of water

It was at this moment that Top US money-earner Curtis Strange lost the 1985 US Masters, at the thirteenth hole, the par 5 which rounds off the tough 'Amen Corner' stretch of the Augusta National course. Strange, comfortably in the lead, hit his second shot into Rae's Creek. With the adrenalin flowing, he felt he could maybe play out and make a birdie.

His recovery shot made contact with the ball, but he watched, agonized, as it rolled back down the slope and almost into the water again. Even as he was dropping a shot, eventual winner Bernhard Langer ahead was making a birdie. Strange never recovered his composure, no doubt pondering why he had not elected to take a penalty drop from the hazard back onto the fairway, then hope to get down in two more for a par 5.

Do not even think of playing out of water if the ball is completely covered. Under most circumstances, the sensible option is to drop out and try to save par. Many golfers forget that when in a hazard you are not allowed to ground the club. This means if you do play out of water, the club must not touch the surface of the water as you prepare to hit the shot.

Hazards like this burn at Augusta are clearly marked. Take care on those occasions when you may not be in the water, but may still be technically in the hazard, that is, inside the markers and cannot, therefore, ground the club.

Mark James
Improvising shots

Ryder Cup golfer Mark James found his ball
lying so badly in this bunker that he could not
get the club to it in the normal way, nor could he
take up a proper stance. It was time to
improvise and he did so brilliantly. With a left-
hand-below-right grip on his wedge, which he
had turned round so that the blade faced
toward rather than away from him, he has
managed left-handed to dislodge the ball. This
is all he could have expected to do.

Sometimes golfers in trouble in the trees turn
the club round in a similar way and punch the
ball out sideways, hitting with a side-saddle
action. Facing away from the target, the shot is
punched down and through the ball, bringing
the club down to the side of the body. Shots like
these take extra concentration, but be assured
that the number of occasions on which you will
have to improvise as Mark James has here are
very few. Remember, too, that sometimes when
you find yourself in a spot where you cannot
swing at the ball, you may be able to knock it
clear with your putter, even if only to move it a
short distance. If there is no way at all to play
the shot, you can move two club lengths clear
of the obstruction but no nearer the hole, or go
back as far as you want on the line of the shot
under penalty of one stroke.

Fred Couples
In the trees

When Fred Couples won the TPC title at
Sawgrass in 1984 he was hardly ever in trouble.
When he did stray off line he was lucky and got
away with it, as here. He had driven his ball into
the high pines, but it lay in a position from
which he could hit a full shot. There is no
restriction on either his take-away or his very
full follow-through. In addition, he was
fortunate enough to have an escape route out
through the trees towards the green, but the
position of his feet indicates a slightly closed
stance and a shot shaped sharply from right to
left.

The golfer who wins will have had his
moments of luck, and this was one of the
escapes Couples made during that tournament.
The great escape artist in recovering from
woods was at one time Seve Ballesteros. He
could thread a ball through a gap as small as
2 square yards (1.7 square metres) and usually
had luck on his side – but remember that Seve is
a golfing wizard. He is now a more controlled
player, however, and far less often needs to play
the dramatic recovery.

Most times when you are in the trees, just
make sure of getting the ball back into play. It
could mean coming out sideways or even
backwards, but that is preferable to being too
ambitious and landing in further trouble. If your
ball hits a tree and rebounds against you, you
have incurred a further penalty and find
yourself still with a difficult shot to play.

Bob Charles
Left-handed play

The greatest left-hander in professional golf comes from a country which has not produced many golf stars. The country is New Zealand and the player Bob Charles, now in his fifties and combining his golf these days with running a successful sheep farm. He has been a star for over 25 years and has won many tournaments around the world, including the New Zealand Open as an amateur in 1954, and the British Open in 1963.

A tall man with an upright swing, Charles's real strength has always been his putter. No-one has had a more deadly putting touch than Bob Charles, who has had more tap-in pars than almost anyone else in golf.

Being left-handed today in golf is no disadvantage, although in the past naturally left-handed golfers were usually persuaded to play right-handed for two reasons. There were few professionals capable of 'turning things around' to teach left-handers and, even more importantly, there were few left-handed clubs on the market. Now all that has changed dramatically. Sets of left-handed clubs are readily available and local pros are far better prepared to give lessons.

If you are a left-handed player, learning from the example of the top golfers, the majority of whom are right-handed, generally means you must mentally reverse the procedures and practise the action independently to develop your own stance and style. Any amateur golfer can follow Bob Charles's example in maintaining fitness – he is careful of his diet – and as for his method, it has always been reliable, the result of much practice. These two factors have helped him stay on top. There is no substitute for hard work when it comes to golfing success!

Wind and rain

Problems in the Walker Cup at Pine Valley in 1985 for Duffy Waldorf and Sam Randolph after heavy rain caused a number of greens to flood. Several areas of casual water have gathered on the green, preventing the Americans from putting to the hole. In such circumstances a golfer is allowed to lift and replace the ball no nearer the hole but on a dry line to it. In this instance, even this solution was not possible and, at the committee's discretion, a caddy is trying to mop up enough of the water to make it possible to putt. Sometimes at professional events huge motor mops are used to clear water from the greens, or squeegees which must not, however, be drawn down the line of a putt. On those occasions when heavy rain causes flooding to occur around the hole during play, officials can cut new holes on higher ground on the green to get the competition completed.

Playing in the rain can be unpleasant and, if you happen to wear spectacles, annoying, too, but it can be equally tough to score well in the high winds that sometimes keep the rain away. It is difficult to stay balanced, especially if the wind is gushing, and not easy to assess club selection when you must play both into the wind and downwind.

In blowy conditions, widen your stance to help you keep your balance. Don't be afraid of the conditions – try to make them work for you. Playing into the wind use one club more, a 4 instead of a 5, for example. Cheat the wind by keeping the shot low and do not lash at it. Try to swing easily at the ball. Downwind you can afford to take a club less because the wind will lift and carry the ball further.

Extremes of weather

Some tournaments are bedevilled each year by bad weather – heavy rain, bitter cold or thick clinging, cold mist that disrupts play and makes conditions tough for golfers and spectators alike. Not that the inclement weather conditions have affected the galleries on this occasion at the World Match-Play at Wentworth – spectators are following the play several deep.

Visibility on this occasion has been just good enough to allow play to continue. Normally in professional events, tournament officials would blow the whistle if the players were unable to see their shots to finish. This is fair when the prize funds these days are so massive. Persistent fog can be a major nuisance, never more so than in Monte Carlo where the Open is staged each year on top of a mountain at Mont Agel, even in summer so often enshrouded in low cloud. The problem is a summer one in southern France and an autumn one in England, but curiously, some amateurs play better in the mist, which hides the hazards and screens the lurking dangers!

In a real frost or under snow, play is unlikely to be allowed on the greens, but sometimes you can get in some practice in less sophisticated style using temporary greens. In cold conditions the ground will be harder, the course slightly faster. It is important to wear warm but not bulky clothing and to protect your hands between shots to keep the sensitivity in your fingers. If you do play in snow, a coloured ball is useful – orange or yellow balls, now readily available are more easily seen in snow and, curiously, are also used in the opposite extremes on grass-less desert courses for better visibility.

Nathaniel Crosby
Young players

Nathaniel Crosby, son of the late Bing Crosby, always dreamed of being a golf professional. Of course, he made sure of gaining a college degree before trying his luck at the American Tour School, where as a former amateur champion he had high hopes of earning his player's card. Earning a Tour Ticket in the USA, however, is far from easy – over 800 players annually try for just 50 tour spots, and Crosby missed out twice. But Nathaniel had made up his mind and put an alternative plan into operation. He travelled to Europe and earned a card to play on the other side of the Atlantic.

There is no particular time at which it is best to start playing golf – Sandy Lyle started at the age of three, but many youngsters take up the game in their early teens. Golf can be a pleasurable and rewarding game at any age, but it is not useful to encourage any young player to believe that professional success is within easy reach. More and more young golfers are turning pro these days in the hope of emulating, by their late twenties, the achievements of Lyle, Langer, Strange, Ballesteros or Faldo – but these men are, of course, the game's most exceptional players. Dozens of young hopefuls never survive their first year on tour, failing to adapt to the different disciplines of pro golf compared to the play-for-fun amateur game. When comparisons were made recently, it was discovered that the golfer who finished fiftieth on the European list was averaging, in amateur terms, scores worthy of a plus-2 handicap! Professional standards are incredibly high and the majority of young players will in the long run get more satisfaction from developing a good amateur game than chasing glory in vain. To be a successful professional you need to have been not just a useful amateur, but a very good one.

Peter Thomson

Playing on

The Senior Circuit, which began in the USA in 1980 with two events and has grown to a 28-tournament circuit worth well over six million dollars in prize money, has given Australian Peter Thomson, five-times winner of the British Open, a new lease of life.

The Senior Tour is attracting as much attention these days as the main US Tour, enjoying its popularity because of the personalities involved. Arnold Palmer and Gary Player are notable Seniors and Lee Trevino is soon to join their ranks. The future for the Over-50s is bright indeed.

Thomson has maintained the excellent swing that made him a world-class player, and note the determination he shows in this shot, which underlines how expert his timing is. The key to Thomson's success has always been good rhythm, but he also has a fierce competitive spirit behind his statesmanlike manner.

One of the main advantages of the game of golf is the fact that it is possible to keep playing long after sportsmen involved in more hectic activities have had to retire. Maybe Thomson and Palmer do not hit the ball quite so hard or so far as they used to; perhaps their putting is less assured, but they still have charisma and personality and, importantly, both players are still very fit.

Continuing fitness is partly a matter of luck as you grow older, but as a rule, those aches and pains don't ease so quickly as before and you may suffer more tiredness towards the end of the round. Be prepared to adopt new standards and modify your game to your own capabilities, but don't give up an activity which gives you such pleasure just because you are no longer quite so fresh or so agile as you once were.

Bob Hope

Older golfers

One of the beauties of golf is that you can play the game from the ages of 3 to 93 or more! Old age in itself is no deterrent as long as you are reasonably fit. In fact, the love of the game and the determination to keep playing has kept many old timers on their feet! Comedian Bob Hope is now into his 80s, but he has been a very good golfer and has retained a basically sound game because he swings through the ball rather than hits at it. His game is a good example of the first rule of golf, which is that it is best to master a good swing before trying to hit the ball hard.

Of course, old age means a more restricted backswing, less shoulder turn and maybe not too much of a follow-through, but entertainer Hope still has plenty of rhythm and manages to accelerate the club through the ball very well.

Bob Hope is lucky in that he plays his golf in reliably warm, sunny weather, whereas other golfers of his age in colder climates find themselves battling the elements. Unkind weather can take some of the pleasure out of playing regularly. To avoid over-exhaustion, older golfers might play a 9-hole rather than an 18-hole game, or follow a looped course around the clubhouse, if such an arrangement is possible. Taking out fewer clubs also reduces the weight you have to carry – unless, like Bob Hope, you have the benefit of an electric buggy to get you around! The reduced number of clubs can present an exciting new challenge in your game, as you will have to learn to manufacture shots much more. Adapt your game and you can continue to enjoy it. No-one else will think any the less of you, so don't put unreasonable demands on yourself.

Kitrina Douglas
Women's golf

British golfer Kitrina Douglas, on being left out of the 1984 Curtis Cup team, decided to turn professional and won her first event – the Ford Classic at Woburn, England. She may not be a long hitter but she succeeds through uncanny accuracy and wise club selection. Kitrina is a member of the women's tour in Europe which has been growing in both prize money and number of tournaments for the past five years. Kitrina and her colleagues travel through Europe to Sweden, France, Spain and Germany during the summer in a tour designed to complement rather than rival the men's circuit. She is seen in action here at La Manga in Spain, one of several golfing complexes visited by European amateur golfers chasing the sun, and regular venue for the European Tour's annual PGA school.

It is often said that male amateur players can learn more from watching the top women professionals than they can from studying Tom Watson or Jack Nicklaus. The terrific power and long hitting of the male golfing stars is generally beyond the range of average players, whereas the women offer a game with less power but excellently judged in rhythm and tempo. This is the main difference between the men's and women's games. A top woman golfer, however skilled and practised, just is not built to generate the same power as her male counterpart. But an easy, smooth swing action in a well-timed swing compensates with both distance and accuracy.

This shot illustrates how well Kitrina is balanced; she has not slid through the shot and although she is now looking towards the target, she would have stayed well down on the hit.

Seaside golf

Seaside golf courses reflect the earliest origins of the game, as a pastime for the shepherds grazing their flocks on the Scottish dunes, using their crooks as makeshift clubs to hit stones or rough balls into rabbitholes. The bunkers on the modern golf course are a throwback to those original conditions on the undulating beachland and now present a variety of golfing hazards.

This picture shows the English course of Royal St George's, venue of the 1985 Open Championship won by Sandy Lyle. Here golfers find one bunker which is over 50 feet (15.3 metres) high. Off a back tee and into the wind, the amateur would find it tough to fly it. One golfer whose ball stuck in the soft sand near the top, climbed up and made an effort to hit it clear. The ball stayed put, but he toppled down and was fortunate not to injure himself.

A command of the chip-and-run shot and the ability to play in wind are essential at seaside links. Because there are few, often no, trees there is no shelter from winds which can be variable in direction and strength even during a round.

Real seaside golf is an art in itself, forcing the golfer to cope with hard, fast-running fairways and lightning fast greens made more difficult to read by the subtle burrows caused by natural humps and hollows. It calls for wind-cheating shots with low trajectories and punched approach shots; it involves clipping the ball from the surface more often, as you cannot take a divot from the hard, sandy ground. There are side-hill, uphill and downhill lies to contend with and these test a golfer's patience as well as skill. That is why the oldest golf championship in the world – the British Open – is always staged on seaside links.

Inland golf

The increasing popularity of golf earlier in this
century encouraged the development of new
broad-ranging courses in locations quite
different from the open seaside venues which
were originally common ground. The modern
game is typically played on land rented or
bought from private individuals or institutions,
making golf club fees more expensive and the
clubs more exclusive.

Naturally, inland courses are distinct in
character from those by the sea. Conditions are
generally less windy but the land itself is often
heavier and the grass less wiry. The major
hazard is likely to be the trees – huge oaks to be
hit round or over, lines of firs to avoid, stands of
silver birch to negotiate. Inland courses have
effectively created a new game, demanding
revised strategies and methods of play.

Many of the great players of the modern
game have become acknowledged golf
architects, designing new courses on parkland
and meadowland, or in woodland through
which the wind whistles tantalizingly. Knowing
the game well, player-architects have been able
to use all the natural features of a location – the
trees, vegetation, lakes and streams – to create
a challenging environment for golf. Holes using
the natural land contours of an inland site can
be far more dramatic than the pleasantly
undulating seaside links. A hole skilfully cut
through the trees offers a remarkable
perspective, looking tighter and narrower than
it really is. Greens built on higher ground,
sometimes jutting out from a hill, make an
approach shot particularly crucial. Golfers
driving off the tee have to think hard about their
chances of flying a cross-fairway brook or
clearing a lake.

Florida golf – American style

Most of the golf courses in the USA – and especially in the southern states, from California and Arizona in the west to through Texas to Florida in the east – are heavily watered and designed to be played by golfers driving electric carts. At first this may seem contrary to the concept of an obvious link between sport and healthy exercise, but it has to be said that temperatures can be 90°F (33°C) and above, and in those circumstances 18 holes are too tiring on foot!

Unlike the courses by the sea in Britain, which are quite natural, American courses are typically artificial. There are exceptions, like the beautiful Pine Valley course in Clementon, New Jersey, but often considerable work is put into landscaping a new course to emulate the open naturalness of seaside links. Since 1960 most new courses in the US have been developed in conjunction with real estate, when the sale of houses discreetly built around the complex pays for the cost of constructing the course. This tends to ensure exclusivity, but there are also, of course, holiday resort courses being built with condominiums and apartments to let, such as the beautiful Wild Dunes on the North Carolina coast. These can provide top-quality year-round golf for holiday makers, with a team of golfing pros on hand to provide instruction and advice.

On man-made courses in the US the grass is often of a coarse variety and must be kept well-watered. This means very little run is possible, and an ability to hit long in the air is a distinct advantage. So much water is required for regular use on the course that the lakes are really reservoirs, like this one at the Sawgrass seventeenth where the green is virtually an island.

Caddies

Caddies are a breed apart. Most of them these days are young, intelligent and resilient, and the very successful travel the world with the golfing stars. A top caddy will be expected to have checked all the pin positions and distances and cleaned the clubs before tee-off. Of course, the caddy can sometimes expect to be asked advice on club selection, although the players mostly decide this for themselves. With rounds taking upwards of four hours it is a long slog, especially in bad weather, carrying a very heavy bag.

For young players starting out, caddying for a more experienced player can be a useful introduction to the ins and outs of the game. Jack Nicklaus used to caddy for his father, and Seve Ballesteros started his career in the caddy's role. For the majority of amateur players, it must be said, a caddy is simply an unnecessary luxury, usually available only if a member of the family can be pressed into service. Mind you, it is a great confidence-boosting tactic to take on an experienced caddy with special knowledge of the course you are playing if you are involved in an important tournament.

Equipment and Preparation

Many people mistakenly believe that golf is an expensive game to play right from the start. Of course, it could be if you decided you first needed to buy a properly matched set of clubs, to kit yourself out with the most luxurious cashmere jerseys and to try to join one of the most exclusive clubs – but it would be foolish to do so.

There is little merit in spending a great deal of money on equipment before you discover whether or not you like the game and can achieve a rewarding level of play, so be sensible. Start with a round or two at your local course, where you might be able to hire a set of clubs. Find out if you have the co-ordination and patience for the game, preferably after having had a lesson or two from the local golf pro. I cannot stress enough the value of the club professional as an adviser – you will enjoy your golf much more if you spend wisely on lessons. Learn the basics before you make your first tentative steps on the course. Only after that should you think about buying your own clubs and joining a golf club.

The professional is again a valuable ally in selecting which clubs are best for you. The length of the shaft, the whippiness or stiffness of them to suit your build and strength are among the considerations he will apply when kitting you out. There are dozens of club models to choose from, in varying designs.

There is no need, of course, to buy a complete 14-club set right away. Initially, pop into your pencil-style bag a 3-wood for use off the tee and off the fairway – this has enough loft (angle) to let you get the ball more easily into the air, an important consideration for the beginner. Add a 3-iron, 5-iron, 7-iron, 9-iron, wedge and putter and you are all set.

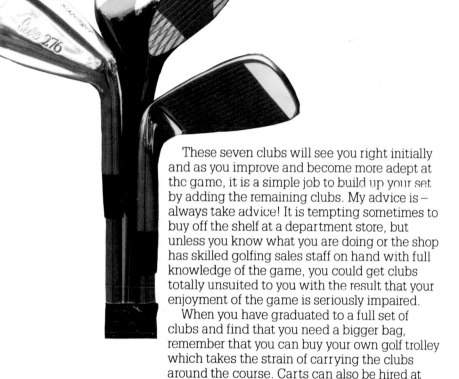

These seven clubs will see you right initially and as you improve and become more adept at the game, it is a simple job to build up your set by adding the remaining clubs. My advice is – always take advice! It is tempting sometimes to buy off the shelf at a department store, but unless you know what you are doing or the shop has skilled golfing sales staff on hand with full knowledge of the game, you could get clubs totally unsuited to you with the result that your enjoyment of the game is seriously impaired.

When you have graduated to a full set of clubs and find that you need a bigger bag, remember that you can buy your own golf trolley which takes the strain of carrying the clubs around the course. Carts can also be hired at most clubs. Some courses have electric carts available although only in the USA are these a regular feature of the golfing scene, as US courses are built for their use. In Britain, for example, few clubs have electric carts and those that do reserve them for over-65s and partly disabled members.

Take note of the ball you play early on. There are varying types – balata and surlyn, solid core and liquid centre. You will note, too, that each non-solid ball has a specific compression, depending on how tightly the rubber inside it is wound. The lower compression ball is best for the amateur. This is easier to hit as it takes a less powerful strike to fire it off the club-head. It is softer than the type used by the professionals who generate such massive club-head speed.

Golf shoes of top quality design guaranteed not to let in the rain are an expensive buy but there are plenty of cheaper models around, maybe not quite so waterproof but effective enough until you decide you want to continue playing seriously – and the same goes for waterproof clothing. Buy the best quality rain gear only after you have decided to give the game a real chance.

Pacing your game

Above all, when you do start to play, do so with a reasonable speed. Nothing spoils the enjoyment of the game more than following a particularly slow group playing out each hole in match-play competition when it is unnecessary after a hole has been won or lost. Match-play is hole-by-hole play in which the golfers win and lose holes until one has an unbeatable advantage – 3-up and two to play, 5-up and four to play, etc. In this game you can pick up after a hole has been won. It is only in stroke play, where the score for each hole is recorded and a final total for 18 holes produced, that you need to hole out all the time.

If you happen to lose your ball you have five minutes to look for it – so do not take longer and before starting the search, wave the next group through. Be as courteous to others on the course as you would want them to be to you. Above all enjoy it. Golf is a great character builder, providing healthy exercise without excessive effort. Maybe the rules are a bit complicated at times, but the interpretation of them in the bar – the nineteenth hole – afterwards provides much stimulating discussion. Remember, it is a game, so do not take it too seriously. It's meant to be fun.

Irons

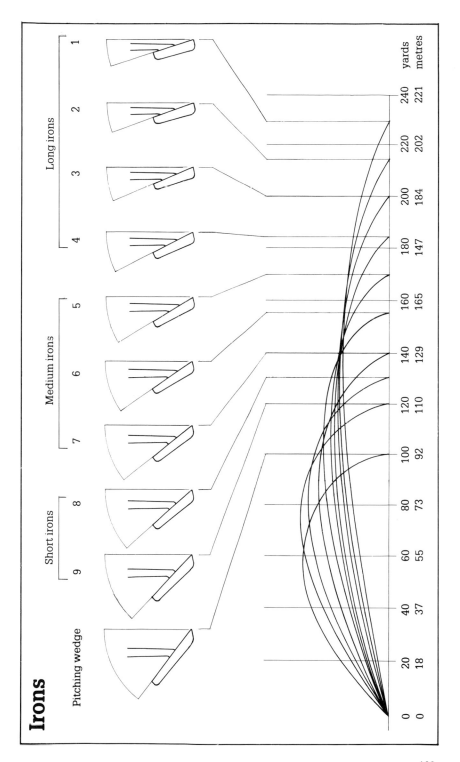

Pitching wedge · Short irons · Medium irons · Long irons

9 8 7 6 5 4 3 2 1

yards	metres
0	0
20	18
40	37
60	55
80	73
100	92
120	110
140	129
160	165
180	147
200	184
220	202
240	221

Fitness Plan

The routine workout

There was a time when it was thought that the best way to get fit was to play a sport. However, for many sports you need first to be fit to play them satisfactorily, and golf is a prime example. What's more, this is a 'one-sided' sport. The same hand directs the power behind the hit each time and the body turns repeatedly from one side to the other. This can lead to niggling aches and strains caused by imbalance in muscle use.

This fitness plan is designed to get you in trim, with a routine for all-round fitness and special exercises of particular benefit to golf players. It is effective, but does not take up too much time, so it can put you in peak condition without diverting the energy you wish to put into playing your sport.

The basic 8-week plan

This consists of three types of activity: pattering and stretching, which occupy a few minutes daily, and additional aerobic exercise, to be fitted into your timetable six days a week.

Pattering is a simple but highly effective way of giving your heart and lungs a thorough workout without putting a strain on your knees and ankles. It also increases agility and speeds up reactions. It is similar to running on the spot but you *do not* lift your knees as if taking running steps. Your feet should barely leave the floor as you patter on the spot as fast as you can.

A fast patter means moving your feet at a rate of about 5 times a second. A few seconds of this pace and a further slower period and you've had enough after a mere minute or so. You'll feel a tightening of the calf muscle at the back of the lower leg at first. This will soon go away.

Stretching is slowly being recognized as one of the most vital ways of both avoiding injury and maintaining the natural spring of your muscles. A simple set of stretching exercises is included here that you can use daily to give your main muscle groups a good workout.

Ease into the stretch, going to the limit of discomfort, holding it a few seconds and then relaxing. Ignore those bouncy enthusiasts who exhort you to leap up and down like a Jack-in-the-Box. *Stretch gently,* like a cat waking up.

Aerobic exercise is slow but sure, the sort of exercise that takes a bit of time but doesn't leave you gasping for breath. It is sustained exercise which causes you to breath deeply and take in oxygen and does not necessarily imply the type of exhaustive routine followed in the modern trend of aerobics classes. The following activities are all aerobic exercise and you can choose one or a combination of any or all as part of your fitness routine.

Walking Set a target; the corner of the street, around the block, to the post office and back. Move briskly and with purpose. Don't combine this with carrying the shopping or stopping to look around.

Jogging/running As above, map out a route and follow it purposefully. Alter the route frequently if you are inclined to lose interest in running for its own sake.

Swimming Swim lengths or widths of a pool and combine this with static in-water exercises, such as holding the side rail and kicking your legs, or hooking feet to the side rail and moving your arms.

Cycling Build up pace and distance gradually as you get fitter.

Dancing Find a class with music you enjoy and people you like, that offers a comprehensive sequence of moves to work on the whole body.

Pace An important part of exercising is quality, not quantity, so the fitness plan suggests only a brief time for each form of exercise. To find out how fast you should go, use the 'talk test'. If you cannot chat to yourself as you work out, you are breathless from working too fast. As you get fitter, you will be able to accommodate a faster pace. This is just as useful as increasing the time you spend.

When to exercise
Use the chart to timetable the routine to your own lifestyle. Take the exercise when your body feels comfortable. Some of us are naturally morning people while others feel more lively in the evening. In fact, you could fit the whole routine into your lunch hour or carry out the pattering and stretching in the morning, the aerobic session at midday or after work.

How to exercise
Remember that exercise is meant to improve your condition, not become an additional strain. Use the following guidelines to make the best use of the fitness routine.

Check with your doctor before embarking on the fitness plan if
- you are over 40
- you have high blood pressure
- you have heart/bone/joint disease
- you suffer from chest pains

Once you start, don't train with friends and family. This tends to turn into competitive rather than shared activity, which puts you under unnecessary stress.

Warm up before doing an exercise routine (and before going out to play golf). Your muscles need oxygen to function efficiently, whatever your degree of fitness, and you will exercise or play better if you're warmed up. What's more, you will lessen the chance of aches, pains and injuries.

After playing or exercising, wind down gently. Never stop suddenly. This also applies *during* exercise. If you feel dizzy, faint or suddenly fatigued, don't immediately flop to the floor or on to a chair — keep moving but slow down gradually to allow your body to change gear.

Maintaining fitness

When you are really pressed for time on your fitness routines, work on the principle 'anything is better than nothing'. Do keep up the daily pattering and stretching even if you cannot fit in aerobic exercise six days a week. Always patter first to ensure that oxygen-rich blood is pumping around your body before you stretch your muscles. Do the 5-minute workout whenever your body feels happiest — or better still, twice a day, once in the morning and once in the evening.

Pattering Follow the pace and timing shown on the chart for your age group (see over).

Stretching Hold each stretch for about 6 seconds. Do each stretch between 8 and 12 times, depending on how fit you feel.

Fitness Plan — 7-Day Routine

DAY	1	2	3	4	5	6	7
PATTERING	1-2 mins daily — increase pace weekly as below						
STRETCHING	Repeat the six exercises daily.						
AEROBIC	5 mins	8 mins	10 mins	15 mins	15 mins	REST	20 mins

Age 15-25 Repeat the 7-day routine over 8 weeks		Age 26-35 Repeat the 7-day routine over 16 weeks		Age 36-50 Repeat the 7-day routine over 24 weeks		Age 50+ Repeat the 7-day routine over 32 weeks
WEEKS 1-2	I	WEEKS 1-4	I	WEEKS 1-3	I	WEEKS 1-4
30 secs slow	N	20 secs slow	N	15 secs slow	N	5 secs slow
15 secs fast	C	10 secs fast	C	10 secs fast	C	5 secs fast
30 secs slow		20 secs slow		15 secs slow		5 secs slow
WEEKS 3-4	R	WEEKS 5-8	R	WEEKS 4-6	R	WEEKS 5-8
30 secs slow	E	30 secs slow	E	20 secs slow	E	5 secs slow
30 secs fast	A	15 secs fast		10 secs fast		10 secs fast
30 secs slow	S	30 secs slow	A	20 secs slow	A	5 secs slow
WEEKS 5-6	E	WEEKS 9-12	S	WEEKS 7-12	S	WEEKS 9-12
30 secs slow		30 secs slow	E	30 secs slow	E	10 secs slow
45 secs fast	P	30 secs fast		15 secs fast		10 secs fast
30 secs slow	A	30 secs slow		30 secs slow		10 secs slow
WEEKS 7-8	T	WEEKS 13-14	P	WEEKS 13-18	P	WEEKS 13-16
30 secs slow	T	30 secs slow	A	30 secs slow	A	20 secs slow
60 secs fast	E	45 secs fast	T	30 secs fast	T	10 secs fast
30 secs slow	R	30 secs slow	T	30 secs slow	T	20 secs slow
	I	WEEKS 15-16	E	WEEKS 19-21	E	WEEKS 17-20
	N	30 secs slow	R	30 secs slow	R	30 secs slow
	G	60 secs fast	I	45 secs fast	I	15 secs fast
		30 secs slow	N	30 secs slow	N	30 secs slow
	P		G	WEEKS 22-24	G	WEEKS 21-24
	A			30 secs slow		30 secs slow
	C		P	60 secs fast	P	30 secs fast
	E		A	30 secs slow	A	30 secs slow
			C		C	WEEKS 25-28
			E		E	30 secs slow
						45 secs fast
						30 secs slow
						WEEKS 29-32
						30 secs slow
						60 secs fast
						30 secs slow

Calf muscle stretch

Stretch out your arms and lean forward with your hands flat against the wall. Keeping feet together and toes pointing forwards, press your hips forwards without bending your knees. Hold the stretch when you feel the pull on your calf muscles.

Hip rotation

Put your hands together and lean forward against a wall, with one leg in front of the other. Push out your hip on the side of the back leg and hold for 10 to 20 seconds. Reverse the position of the legs and repeat on the other side.

Trunk rotation

Stand with feet apart and planted in line with your shoulders. Clasp your fingers in front of you with elbows out to the sides. Turn from the hip, pushing back as far as possible to one side without moving your feet. Repeat to the other side.

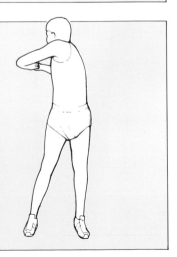

Adductor (inner thigh) stretch

Stand upright with feet apart. Keeping your upper body straight, bend one knee forward and hold the stretch when you feel a pull in the straightened leg. Repeat, bending the other leg forward.

Side stretch

Raise both arms over your head and clasp your hands. Bend sideways from the waist, without leaning forwards. Press gently to the side but do not strain as you stretch. Repeat to the other side.

Calf, quadriceps and hip stretch

Stand upright with hands on hips and lunge forward, behind your front leg and dropping your weight onto it. You should feel a 'pull' in the thigh of your rear leg. Hold the stretch for 10 seconds. Return to upright position and repeat with the other leg forward.

Golf Fitness Exercises

Once you have raised your general level of fitness you need to work on the specific areas of your body used in hitting a golf ball. For example, many golfers want to add length to their drives, but this involves strengthening arm, shoulder and back muscles, so all the following exercises are important. What's more, with the amount of walking you do, especially on hilly courses, leg strength (or lack of it) shows as you reach the end of a round. If the legs, heart and lungs tire, then your timing will falter, throwing out your technique.

Although a strong upper body helps, it is fitness allied to technique which produces confidence, and success in any sport is all about confidence. Of course you can pick out one or two of the following exercises to strengthen flabby areas of your body, but don't ignore your overall needs. No gymnasium is needed; do the exercises at home or in spare moments during the working day.

GRIP EXERCISE
Strengthens wrist and forearm

Lessens/prevents occurrence of wrist and elbow problems

Use a ball, the size of a tennis ball but softer. Squeeze it 12 times in each hand. Hold each squeeze for 5 full seconds. Do not overdo this as you could then *cause* forearm problems. Build up to a maximum of 20 squeezes a day, over about four weeks.

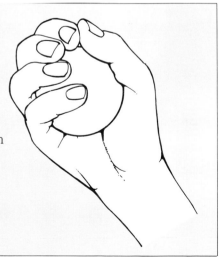

PRESS UPS
Strengthen arms, shoulder and chest muscles

Lessen/prevent incidence of shoulders and high back pains

With all press ups, breathe out as you go down; breathe in as you come up again. Go up and down — *don't* hold the bent arm position.

Move from exercise 1 up to exercise 3 as you increase in strength and fitness. Start with the first exercise and do 8 each day. Work up to 20 a day after about four weeks. Then move up to the second exercise, then to the third. 20 a day is quite sufficient for exercise 3.

1 Kneel on all fours, arms shoulder-width apart, hands placed slightly in front of shoulders. At first, just touch forehead to floor. When stronger, move hands further forward and touch chest to floor. This is quite easy as your hands and knees take the weight when you push up.

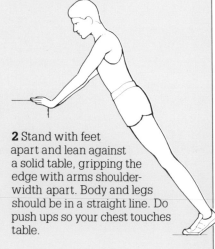

2 Stand with feet apart and lean against a solid table, gripping the edge with arms shoulder-width apart. Body and legs should be in a straight line. Do push ups so your chest touches table.

3 Do proper press ups, supported on your hands and toes with knees and torso leaving the floor. Keep your back straight and head in comfortable position, not thrust back awkwardly.

ABDOMINAL EXERCISE

Strengthens
abdominal muscles

**Together with Neck
and Shoulder
exercises, prevents
back complaints,
particularly lower
back**

Move from exercise 1 up to exercise 3
as you increase in strength and
fitness.

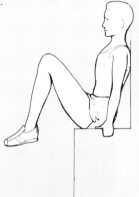

1 Lie flat on your back, arms by your side. Bring your knees up into a comfortable bend. Lift your head, shoulders and upper back slightly off the ground. Do 8 times a day. Build up to 20 times a day over about four weeks.

2 Sit on the front edge of a plain, kitchen-type chair. Grip the sides of the chair, just behind your body. Lean back so that your shoulders touch the back of the chair. Now try to touch your kneecaps to your forehead, bringing both your head forward and your legs up. Do 8 times a day. Build up to 20 times a day over about four weeks.

3 Lie on your back, arms by your sides and do the traditional 'sit up', trying to touch your toes. Do 5 times a day. Build up to 20 times a day over about four weeks.

NECK AND SHOULDER EXERCISES

Strengthen neck, shoulders, upper back

Lessen/prevent aches and pains in neck, shoulders and triceps strain

Do each of these exercises 6 times, holding each push or pull for 5 seconds. Build up to a maximum of 20 a day, after about four weeks.

1 With elbows out horizontally, place hands on forehead. Try to push your head backwards with your hands, at the same time pushing forwards with your head.

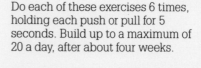

3 With elbows out horizontally, grip hands together. Then try to pull them apart.

2 With elbows out horizontally, clasp hands behind head. Push forwards with hands, backwards with head.

4 With elbows out horizontally, put the palms of your hands together. Push them together hard.

LEG EXERCISES
**Strengthen 'quads',
the big group of
muscles on front of
thigh**

**Take stress off knee
joint, minimizing
injury**

1 Standing up or lying in bed, try to
press knee 'backwards' with leg in
straight position. Hold press for
10 seconds. Build up to 50 a day.

All leg muscles except quadriceps
are well-catered for by pattering and
aerobic exercise of your choice
though cycling *does* workout this
important muscle group.

2 Do short 'shuttle runs' over 5 yds
(5m) where you sprint, bend down
and pick up small bean bag, heavy
plastic bottle — any object that's
easy to pick up and weighs about
2 lbs (1 kg). Do 6 times. Build up to
20, even 30 over a month. This not
only lessens the occurrence of knee
injuries but is also good for the lower
back and for general agility.

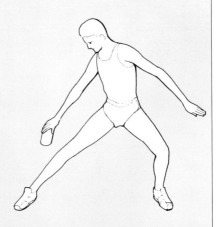